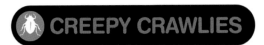

The Life Cycle of
Army Ants

New Forest Press

An Hachette Company

First published in the United States by
New Forest Press, an imprint of Octopus Publishing Group Ltd

www.octopusbookusa.com

Copyright © Octopus Publishing Group Ltd 2012

Published by arrangement with Black Rabbit Books
PO Box 784, Mankato, MN 56002

Library of Congress Cataloging-in-Publication Data

Twist, Clint.
The Life Cycle of Army Ants / by Clint Twist.
p. cm. -- (Creepy Crawlies)
Includes index.
Summary: Describes the life of an army ant by explaining its body parts, habitat, and behaviors. Explains how the army ants work together in a colony to find food, care for the young, and protect the queen ant. Compares the army ant to other ants and insects. Includes life-cycle diagram and close-up photos of body parts--Provided by publisher.
ISBN 978-1-84898-517-9 (hardcover, library bound)
1. Army ants--Life cycles--Juvenile literature. I. Title.
QL568.F7T857 2013
595.79'6--dc23
2012003594

Printed and bound in the USA

16 15 14 13 12 1 2 3 4 5

Publisher: Tim Cook   Editor: Margaret Parrish   Designer: Steve West

Picture credits:
b=bottom; c=center; t=top; r=right; l=left
Alamy: 19t (Danita Delimont), 19 side panel (Soren Breiting). Alex Wild (www.myrmecos.net):
2-3, 4, 4-5, 5, 5 side panel, 8-9, 10, 17 side panel, 19b. FLPA: 8, 16 (Norbert Wu/Minden Picture),
9 side panel, 13b (Mark Moffett/Minden Pictures). Getty Images: 25b (George Grall). NHPA: 9t
(George Bernard), 23 (Adrian Hepworth). OSF: 16-17. Premaphotos Wildlife: 1, 15 side panel
(Ken Preston-Mafham). Science Photo Library: 12 (Mona Lisa Production),13 side panel
(Dr. Morley Read), 15t, 21 (George Bernard), 14-15 (Sinclair Stammers), 26 (Jean-Phillipe Varin/
Jacana), 7 side panel (Volker Steger).

Contents

What is an Army Ant?

Army ants are small insects. They march in vast numbers, with more than a million in a single column.

Army ants are carnivores—they eat other animals, mainly insects. They are predators that hunt, catch, and kill their prey. They are also scavengers and feed on the bodies of dead animals.

Army ants live in the tropical forests of South and Central America and Africa. African army ants are called driver ants.

An army ant soldier

Ants are called social insects because they live in large families known as colonies.

Army ants live and work together in the colony.

Who's Who?

Insects belong to a group of animal known as arthropods. Adult arthropods have jointed legs, but no inner skeleton. Instead, they have a tough outer exoskeleton. All insects have six legs when they are adults, and most adult insects have wings and use either one pair or two pairs for flight.

All ants are arthropods.

Up Close and Personal

An army ant worker is about ½ in (1.5 cm) long with very thin legs and no wings. Its outer covering (exoskeleton) is tough.

An army ant is an insect and therefore has three body sections: head, thorax, and abdomen.

The head contains the brain, mouth, and antennae. Some army ants have eyes, but most are blind.

Close-up of the head

The abdomen is largest part of the body and contains the stomach and other important organs.

Six Legs

Insects are sometimes called hexapods because they have six legs ("hex" means six in Latin). All insects are hexapods, but not all hexapods are insects. Springtails, for instance, have six legs but are not true insects.

The thorax is the thinnest part of the body. The ant's three pairs of legs are attached here.

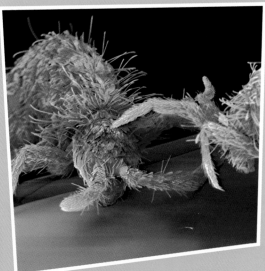

Don't let the leg count fool you. This springtail isn't an insect.

Roving Colony

An insect colony is one big family of related insects. A large colony can contain 20 million ants, but most have fewer than 2 million.

These ants are sweeping the forest floor for prey.

A single army ant eats a tiny amount of food daily. If you add up all the food needed for each ant, however, it is a huge amount. To feed its appetite, the colony is always hunting for food. If it stops, it will quickly starve and die.

A colony at rest in a hollow tree

The ants march on a schedule. Fifteen days of nonstop marching is followed by 20 days of rest.

Full of Life

The tropical forests of Central and South America and Africa are packed with life. More species live in these forests than anywhere else on Earth. Hot, wet forests are the only places that produce enough food for army ants, which is why they make them their home.

Army ants devouring a cricket

Ants attacking a tiger moth

Family Members

Every colony contains four types of army ant. Three types—queen, worker, and soldier—are always part of the colony. A fourth type—the male—only appears at certain times.

Each colony contains one fertile female—the queen. At 1 to 2 in (2.5 to 5 cm) long, she is the largest ant in the colony. Her job is to lay eggs.

This worker ant is taking a ride on the queen.

Most other full-time members of the colony are sterile females, known as workers. Their job is to gather food for the colony.

Soldier army ants have eyes so they can detect predators and prey.

Soldiers are large female ants. They can be 1 in (2.5 cm) long and have special weapons for killing prey and defending the workers and queen. Other than the queen, they are the only ants in the colony that can see.

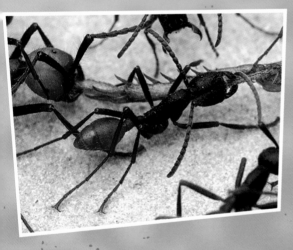

Most ants in the colony are worker ants.

Fierce Fighters

Soldiers are bigger and stronger than workers, and they are equipped with weapons. Their heads and jaws are huge, and they attack in a fearsome head-on charge. Some species have a stinger, while others can squirt poisonous acid.

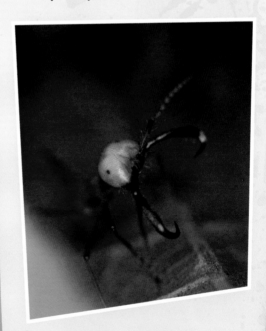

Protect and defend!

Blind Obedience

Army ant workers are blind. They sense their surroundings through vibrations in their legs and by smelling with their antennae.

The ants' antennae detect chemicals called pheromones that are made by other ants in the colony. Because soldier ants can see, they lead scout parties in search of food. When the scouts find food, they lay a trail of pheromones back to the colony. Workers follow the trail and bring back the food.

The blue circle in the center of the head is this soldier ant's eye.

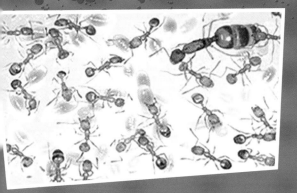

Ants use pheromones to communicate.

If the workers encounter problems (like a predator with a taste for ants), they release alarm pheromones and the soldiers come to their rescue.

Command Central

The queen controls the activity of the colony using "command pheromones" that only she can make. Some commands tell the scouts to search for food, while others say it is time to stop and rest.

Army ants can attack a creature as big as a tarantula.

The queen commands the colony to rest.

Raiding Parties

When the ants are on the move, the whole colony marches through the forest like a living river, eating everything in its path.

When the colony stops, only the raiding party goes out. Raiding parties can contain 600,000 insects.

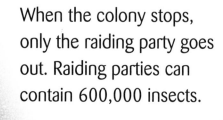

Stealing the larva of a pavement ant

Worker ants tear apart a gryllid cricket

Raiding parties search in a different direction each day, until all available food is found. The colony then moves on.

Army ants eat any animal tissue—living or dead—but their favorite food is termites and other ant species, especially the eggs and larvae. Some army ants steal the eggs of other ants and raise them as workers.

Food Processing

Workers may be blind, but they are extremely efficient at finding food. They work together to carry prey that is too heavy for one ant. They can also cut up prey with their jaws and bring it back to the colony piece by piece.

Taking prey back to the nest

15

Close Community

When they come to a stop, the ants link their bodies to form a living home that can cling to any surface.

Army ants do not need much shelter from the weather, because they provide their own. All the colony needs is a branch or fallen log that can support the combined weight of a million or so ants.

Army ants can use their bodies to build a bridge for other ants.

Army ants build nests by linking their bodies together.

Construction starts with the strongest ants: the soldiers. They grab each other to make chains. Thousands of workers fill the gaps around the outside of the colony. Inside the nest, more ants link their bodies to make spaces for the queen and the eggs. The fiercest soldiers guard the outside.

River Crossing

Ants cannot swim, but that does not stop them from crossing streams and rivers. Soldiers and workers link their bodies to create a "living bridge" across a small stream. They can also build "living rafts" to float the colony across bigger waterways.

By building a bridge with their bodies, army ants can cross any gap in their path.

Army ant nest

Queen Ant

The queen is the most important ant in the colony. All the others can be replaced, but there is just one queen. Her job is to lay eggs that will hatch into new workers.

A queen army ant mates only once, at the beginning of her adult life. She does not lay eggs while the colony is moving, only when it is at rest.

The ants lie one on top of the other to protect the eggs in the nest.

The queen emits a special pheromone while laying eggs so the colony knows to stay put. As soon as the egg-laying ends, she stops making the pheromone, and the colony moves on.

When a colony becomes too big, the queen lays special queen and male eggs. The males and new queens leave to form new colonies.

Flying Ants

Queens and males are the only army ants with wings. The queens fly off to mate and establish new colonies. After a queen has mated, she chews her wings off because she no longer needs them. Males ready to mate go in search of queens. These males are so big they are sometimes called "sausage flies." The males die shortly after mating.

A male sausage fly

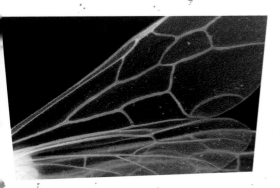

The wing of a male army ant

Raising Young

Army ants take good care of their young. Workers spend as much effort looking after the young as they do collecting food.

Each egg is cared for by a worker ant at all times.

These worker ants are carrying larvae while the soldiers guard them.

Worker ants transport larvae and pupae across the forest floor

When the eggs hatch, the workers do everything for the larvae. They even chew their food so it is easy for them to digest.

After the larvae have become adults they can feed themselves and begin working for the colony.

Development

Insects develop from eggs in two ways. With many insects, including ants, the eggs hatch into larvae that look different from the adults. The larvae go through a stage called metamorphosis, when they change into adults. With other kinds of insect, such as cockroaches and grasshoppers, the eggs hatch into nymphs that have adult body shapes.

The stages of life

Army Ants and Humans

The idea of army ants is scary—an unstoppable mass of insects marching through the forest eating everything in its path. Despite their reputation, however, army ants are not harmful to humans.

Even when walking slowly, humans are faster than army ants, so can easily move out of their way.

Army ants invading a home

Scorpion prey

Trapped animals, such as chickens in coops or goats tied to the ground, are in big trouble. The ants swarm over them and begin feeding. The victims usually die from blood loss.

People in tropical regions actually welcome the arrival of army ants. The ants eat insect pests and dead insects hidden in corners of rooms and under furniture. The visiting ants "spring clean" the home.

Welcome Disturbance

The arrival of an army ant colony is good news for some animals. As the ants approach, many large insects, such as cockroaches and beetles, come out of hiding and try to run away. They may be able to outrun the ants, but larger predators can catch them. Some birds follow army ants and prey on the insects trying to escape them.

The bicolored antbird follows army ants.

A hunt in progress

Different Behaviors

Army ants are always on the move, but other woodland ant species are more settled.

Wood ants

Wood ants get their name because they live in forests in regions where the climate is warm. Wood ants build their nests underground, beneath the forest floor. Nests are made of leaves. In cooler regions, they often construct a mound above the nest. Mounds can be 3 ft (1 m) tall.

Acacia ants

In areas that are too dry for thick forest, some ants build their nests at the base of the thorny acacia trees. The ants feed on the tree's nectar and keep it clear of other insects. If another animal tries to eat the acacia, the ants drive it away.

Leafcutter ants

Leafcutter ants chew off pieces of leaves and carry them back to their nest. The leaves grow a fungus that provides the ants with a steady supply of food.

Aphid-milking ants

Many plants attract aphids, which are small sapsucking insects that produce honeydew. Garden ants stroke aphids while they are feeding, which makes them produce the sticky-sweet honeydew that the ants love to eat.

Unusual Ants

There are about 10,000 species of ant. Most of them are instantly recognizable as ants, but some are not.

Replete ants

Bees are not the only insects that make honey. Some ant species collect nectar and feed it to special workers known as repletes. Repletes store excess food and regurgitate it for other ants to eat. A replete ant can be as big as a grape.

Velvet ant

Despite its name, this "ant" is a wasp that sneaks into bumblebee colonies to lay its eggs. When the wasp eggs hatch, the wasp larvae eat the bee larvae.

Argentine ant

During the last 100 years, Argentine ants have spread all over the world. They are native to South America, but were accidentally introduced into other regions, where they have become pests.

Fire ant

Fire ants were once found only in the forests of South America, but they were brought to other countries in shipments of lumber. They are now serious pests. Fire ant venom is strong enough to kill small animals.

Find Out More

Life Cycle

Army ant eggs are microscopic and white or yellowish in color. The eggs hatch into larva, which do not have eyes or legs. The larva builds a cocoon around itself and changes into a pupa. When the pupa leaves its cocoon, it becomes an adult ant.

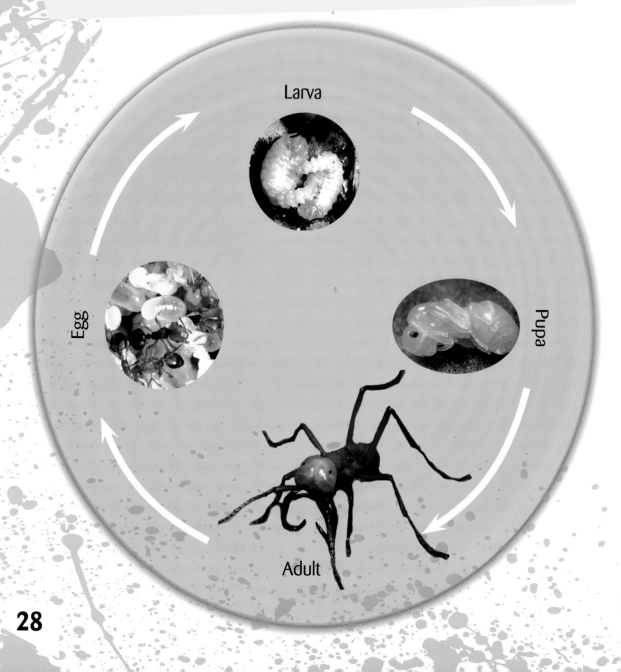

Larva

Egg

Pupa

Adult

Fabulous Facts

Fact 1: A colony of army ants kills and eats up to 100,000 animals (mostly insects) a day!

Fact 2: Army ants can climb trees and eat birds.

Fact 3: The queen only needs to mate once to produce eggs for the rest of her life.

Fact 4: After a male army ant mates with the queen, he dies within 48 hours.

Fact 5: Workers only live for several months, while the queen may live for several years.

Fact 6: Army ants can deliver a painful sting, but they do not come into contact with humans very often.

Fact 7: Army ants have been known to kill and eat an animal as large as a horse!

Fact 8: If you gathered together all the humans in the world and all the ants they would weigh about the same.

Fact 9: In some species of driver ant the queen produces up to four million eggs every month.

Fact 10: Army ants can only swallow liquids; they have to spit out solid food.

Fact 11: The army ant existed during the Age of the Dinosaurs, 100 million years ago. It hasn't really changed since then.

Fact 12: There are about 150 species of army ant. They are found mostly in Central and South America.

Fact 13: Army ants travel at about 3 ft (1 m) per minute when they are marching.

Glossary

Abdomen—the largest part of an insect's three-part body; the abdomen contains many important organs.

Antennae—a pair of special sense organs found at the front of the head on most insects.

Arthropod—a creepy crawly that has jointed legs; insects and spiders are arthropods.

Carnivore—an animal that eats meat.

Caterpillar—a butterfly or moth larva.

Colony—a group of insect or other living thing that lives very closely together.

Cycle—a series of repeated events that follow a regular pattern.

Digestive system—the organs that are used to process food.

Driver ants—a type of army ant that lives in Africa.

Formic acid—substance produced by some ants that causes skin irritation and chemical burns.

Exoskeleton—a hard outer covering that protects and supports the bodies of some insects.

Honey—sweet, syrupy substance produced by honey bees and some ants.

Insect—a kind of creepy crawly that has six legs; most insects also have wings.

Larva—a wormlike creature that is the juvenile (young) stage in the life cycle of many insects.

Nectar—a sweet, sugary substance produced by flowering plants and used by honey bees and some ants to make honey.

Nymph—the juvenile (young) stage in the life cycle of insects that do not produce larvae.

Organ—a part of an animal's body that performs a particular task; for instance, the heart pumps blood.

Parasite—any living thing that lives or feeds on or in the body of another living thing.

Pedicel—the narrow "waist" of an ant at the top of the abdomen where it meets the thorax.

Predator—an animal that hunts and eats other animals.

Prey—an animal that is eaten by other animals.

Pupa—the pupa represents the stage in the life cycle of some insects in which the body of a mature larva is transformed into an adult insect.

Pupation—the process by which insect larvae change their body shape into the adult form.

Queen—the largest army ant in a colony; the queen is the only army ant that can lay eggs.

Regurgitate—to bring up partially digested food.

Replete—a special kind of ant worker that stores honey inside its body.

Scavenger—an animal that eats dead and rotting plants and animals.

Skeleton—an internal structure of bones that supports the bodies of animals such as mammals, reptiles, and fish.

Soldier—a sterile female army ant that is larger than a worker; most soldiers have weapons such as stingers to attack prey and defend the colony.

Thorax—the middle part of an insect's body, where the wings and legs are attached.

Tropical—belonging to the region around the Earth's equator where the climate is always hot.

Worker—a sterile female army ant; nearly all the army ants in a colony are workers.

Index